Debt Free by 30 & Beyond

Ebony At Peace

Published by: Damon Thomas

Editor: Latasha (Fabra laJor) Smith

Graphic Design: Camille Daly

Email: thomas.damonproductions@gmail.com

Copyright: 2014

Debt Free by 30 & Beyond
Ebony At Peace (Ebony Barrier)
DT Productions

All rights reserved. No part of this publication may be reproduced, stored in a retrieval system, or transmitted in any form by any means electronic, mechanical, photocopy, recording, or otherwise. Ebony At Peace (Ebony Barrier) owns all rights to her story, and publication.

Important Publisher's Note:

Many of the names in this story have been changed to protect those who wish not to be identified. The author, Ebony At Peace, also takes complete and ALL legal responsibility for any breach of private identity if/as requested by persons mentioned in this book. The publisher, Damon Thomas, has not contributed whatsoever to its content, except copyediting. The publisher is legally free of any and ALL claims of responsibility regarding the content and the persons described, referred to (implied or explicit), or written about herein.

This publication is designed to provide accurate and authoritative information in regard to the subject matter covered. It is published with the understanding that the publisher and author are not engaged in rendering, legal, accounting, or other professional services. If legal advice or other professional advice, including financial, is required, other services of a competent professional person should be sought.

TABLE OF CONTENTS

Purpose

Acknowledgements

Dedication

Introduction

Chapter 1: Hard Work Pays Off

Chapter 2: Employment Begins

Chapter 3: Life in Debt: The Beginning

Chapter 4: Fired

Chapter 5: Single Motherhood

Chapter 6: Nursing Career Begins

Chapter 7: The Start of Gambling

Chapter 8: Revelation

Chapter 9: Cycle of Abuse

Chapter 10: The Start of "At Peace"

Chapter 11: The "American Dream"

Chapter 12: Financial Slavery

Chapter 13: Words of Wisdom

Chapter 14: What is Debt? **Chapter 15:** The System

Chapter 16: Money Lenders

Chapter 17: Student Loans

Chapter 18: Home Buying

Chapter 19: Car Loans

Chapter 20: Bankruptcy

Chapter 21: Slave-Like Mentality

Chapter 22: Change Your Thought Process

Chapter 23: Self-Satisfaction

Chapter 24: Budget, Budget, Budget

Chapter 25: Steps to a Healthy Budget.

Chapter 26: Ways to Save Money

Chapter 27: Discipline

Chapter 28: The Power of Tithing

Chapter 29: The Financial Side of Your Relationship

Chapter 30: Knowing One's Self

Chapter 31: Breaking Addictions

Chapter 32: Our Children, Our Future

Chapter 33: Life After Debt

Chapter 34: You Can be Debt Free

Purpose

"Debt Free by 30 & Beyond" was written with the intent to teach, encourage, and develop awareness regarding the causes and effects of debt. In today's society, many individuals were taught to believe that debt is a common denominator in the equation of life. According to the national debt clock (as of August 15, 2014 11:15:40 PM GMT Brillig.com), the outstanding public debt is seventeen trillion, six hundred seventy-four billion, one hundred sixty-one million, nine hundred ninety-five thousand, seven hundred ninety-seven dollars, and ninety cents ($17,674,161,995,797.90). The estimated population of the United States is three hundred eighteen million, eight hundred twenty-one thousand, seven hundred fifty- three ($318,821, 753). Therefore, each citizen shares approximately fifty-five thousand four hundred thirty-five dollars and eighty-seven cents ($55,435.87) worth of debt. Isn't there something wrong with this picture? Absolutely, and it's referred to as financial slavery, Galatians 5:1: *"It is for freedom that Christ has set us free. Stand firm then, and do not let yourselves be burdened again by a yoke of slavery."* By sharing my story of how I stumbled into debt and my testimony of how I became completely debt free by the age of thirty, I hope to enlighten and encourage the reader to begin walking the path towards a debt free lifestyle. I'm here to tell you that I am no longer a member of that group of statistics and by sharing my journey, I want to inspire you to work towards severing your membership too. There isn't anything positive about debt. Debt causes people to act out of character, lie, cheat, steal, become drug and alcohol abusers, gambling addicts, and suicidal. Debt can cause health problems such as high blood pressure, depression, and stress. This can cause fear of the unknown and lead to insecurities. Debt is the number one cause for break ups, separations, and divorces. Simply put, debt is a silent killer that affects anything that crosses its path. The major problem about debt is that most of us are unaware of how we've allowed ourselves to fall victim to its preconceived power. Society would also have us believe that debt will follow us for the rest of our lives, as if it was something we were born with. This causes many individuals to become fearful of what the future may hold. I am here to tell you that you are not bound by debt. Take off your rose colored glasses, open your eyes, and see debt for what it really is; just another four-letter word. Many people complain – excessively- about finances, but they fail to seek out solutions to solve the problem. It is time to stand together and build a financially healthy society as a whole. The only way to accomplish this is by shedding light on what habits may have contributed to the manifestation of debt in our lives and how to take the proper steps to remove this tumor. We were not designed to live in debt; that is biblical. By the word of God, debt is corrupt and it has the ability to ruin anyone's life. The Lord has not ordained us to live with debt. He is entirely against it, and we should be too.

ACKNOWLEDGEMENTS

I give all praise and honor to the Lord, my heavenly and almighty Father, for allowing me to become a living testimony. Thank you for leading me to the right path and guiding me every step of the way. A heartfelt thanks to my mother -Sheila Stroud- for sharing her life experiences and raising my brother and me as a single mother. Thanks for showing me love and support through all of my trials and tribulations. To both of my grandmothers, Claudine Jackson and Joan Thirst, thank you for sharing your wisdom and expertise. To my brother, Javelle Howell, thank you for listening to my stories and sharing your experiences in life. To my beautifully gifted son -Calvion Brown- thank you for being my motivation, I could not have gone through this journey of life without you. Thank you, Olynthia (Calvion's Godmother), Diane Whitfield, and family for being there for me and my family and assisting me with raising Calvion; I love you two as a sister and a second mom. To Jarvis Perry, thank you for being with me, sharing my visions, believing in me, and being a role model for my son. Thank you to my auntie, Tracey Allen, for always loving me unconditionally and sharing in the celebration of my accomplishments. To Yemmy Vadis, thank you for being my partner with the birth of "At Peace Health Care Agency." To my former pastor, Pastor Keith Hayward of Lamott AME Church, thanks for encouraging me to follow through with my dreams. To my current pastor, Pastor Louis P. Attles of Lamott AME Church, thank you for listening to my ideas, pastoring me, sharing your ideas, and words of wisdom. A special thanks to my publisher, Damon Thomas, and his team for believing in my project and assisting me with their writing talents and expertise.

DEDICATION

This book is dedicated to my one and only son, Calvion Brown. Take this as your guide and carry on my legacy of striving to live a debt free, financially healthy, and wealthy life.

I LOVE YOU

ALWAYS AND FOREVER

INTRODUCTION

Do you ever.........

- Imagine living a debt free lifestyle?

- Desire to wake up and ask yourself "How will I enjoy my money today?"

- Get frustrated when your paycheck is deposited and, by the time you pay all of your bills, there isn't enough money left over to do the things you want versus the things you need to do?

- Feel that you are being held back from the job you want or living your best life because the debt you've accumulated has lowered your credit score?

- Experience having a financial emergency and have to use credit cards or personal loans instead of paying cash because you don't have any money saved?

- Feel trapped after traveling on borrowed money from credit cards or cash advances that you have to work extra hours to pay off?

- Get tired of making extravagant purchases (you can't afford) to impress others, even though the act is causing you to fall deeper into debt?

Galatians 6:4 (NIV) "Each one should test their own actions. Then they can take pride in themselves alone, without comparing themselves to someone else."

- Get yourself involved with gambling, or any other addiction, to escape your reality (thinking it would make things better) but it actually made things worse?

- Grow tired of drowning in debt from student loans?

- Feel like the education you have isn't paying the salary that you deserve or desire?
- Feel like your dream is turning into your worst nightmare?

- Imagine being in a financially healthy and loving relationship?

- Ask yourself if the purpose of your life consists of working nonstop without being able to enjoy it?

- Realize that being in debt can be unattractive because of the changes it can cause to your character, attitude towards others, and the possibility of looking irresponsible to your children (which can cause them to practice the same bad habits)?

If you've answered yes to any of these questions, then continue to read and learn how I began seeking solutions by operating in my faith, believing in myself, recognizing my spending flaws, learning how to save for -unexpected- events, and eventually becoming debt free.

Chapter 1: Hard Work Pays Off

My mother was a hard worker, period. She worked her fingers to the bone to support our family. But even though we've struggled, we were still able to live a decent life (with the help of our grandmother). I remember when a group of us would go trick or treating. We would always visit upscale neighborhoods like Amherst, NY. I would often peek into the windows of the homes and imagine my family living in someplace that beautiful. That thought was short-lived, because reality was much stronger then my tiny imagination. It angered me; I envied those families because I wanted what they had. Life seemed unfair. Then I quickly found out that Amherst, NY wasn't as wonderful as I'd thought; there was more. Our family began traveling to different parts of the U.S. Bi-annually, we would attend our family reunions in different cities and travel other times during the year, which is when I started noticing different ways of life. Disney World, cruises, theme parks, it was all so new to me, but once I got a taste of something different, that was the life I yearned for. From those experiences, the hustler in me was birthed. That is when I finally understood my mother's saying...HARD WORK PAYS OFF.

Chapter 2: Employment Begins

My first job was working as a telemarketer; I was fifteen. It wasn't a summer youth program, it was a regular job for a firm that sold Triple A (AAA) memberships and magazine subscriptions. At the time, I was one of the youngest employees there. It was definitely a hustle, but I was a hustler (remember). I began receiving awards and recognition for doing my job well. I hit my targeted goals every week and I, eventually, became team leader. The day I received my first paycheck, my grandmother took me to the bank to open a savings account. She taught me all about saving money, but I wasn't mature enough to understand its importance. I was in the mind frame of wanting to buy expensive clothes and shoes because I wanted to look fly at school. My mind was on the "here and now." I barely thought about my future and I seldom thought about college. Actually, thoughts about my future were cloudy. I wanted to live a fairytale life and find a husband who would take care of me like Cinderella. My dreams of my knight in shining armor coming to rescue me and take my hand in marriage began to shatter when I witnessed what many women around me were going through, but I still kept up hope. I learned that two four letter words, LOVE and LIFE, at times, weren't fair, but I watched these women stand strong and never give up. I've witnessed my family, frivolously, spending money on material things that established social status, rather than a financial future. They never spoke of assets such as stocks and bonds, money market accounts, or real estate. I began working two jobs at sixteen; I'd developed a taste for earning money, so my hustle became stronger.

CHAPTER 3: LIFE IN DEBT: THE BEGINNING

At the age of sixteen, I bought my first car, an '88 Ford Bronco. I spent four hundred dollars on it and never got a chance to drive it because it was a lemon. Sure, when I bought the car it was really rusty, but I thought I could fix it up and make it into something fabulous, and of course, I was wrong. When I was seventeen, I bought an old white Chevy Corsica. This was my second car but my first car note. I put a hundred dollars down and paid one hundred and fifty dollars every two weeks until it was paid off. The car was only worth twenty five hundred dollars but (after the interest), I ended up paying a little over four thousand dollars. This was swindling at its finest. Then, at eighteen years old, I received my first credit card and I was able to buy more clothes and shoes (that I couldn't afford) just to keep up with the Joneses. I wanted to be the pretty girl who had all the fly gear. Little did I know, those hundred dollar purchases carried an interest rate of over 22 percent. I can remember my mom telling me *"Don't mess your credit up,"* but I was young and I didn't understand what that really meant. Although it wasn't a detailed conversation, she was sharing wisdom that I later learned was very valuable. I didn't know anything about assets or investing, but I easily learned how to rack up debt like it was second nature. After opening up one credit card, I opened up another and then started opening up several more (including store cards). I thought that I was the most stylishly dressed girl on Earth. I was spending the bulk of my money on material possessions and failed to save some of the money that I worked very hard to earn (sounds familiar?). My senior year of high school, I began looking at various trade schools and a few colleges in Atlanta, but I was still confused about a major. I graduated with the title of Salutatorian and was offered a permanent job straight out of high school. It was a position at Fisher-Price making twenty five thousand dollars a year, plus overtime, and I accepted. Talking to my older co-workers, I began learning about 401ks and investing. But being young gives you this mentality of living in the present and not considering the future. I failed to understand what they were trying to teach me, so I continued to perform the habits I was used to: work, buy, and spend. This time, I was able to save a little because of the automatic deductions from my paychecks going towards my 401k and retirement plan. I traded in my Corsica for a brand new Pontiac Vibe and a larger car note. This time, I was paying five hundred dollars, plus insurance, a month. This was another liability that was unnecessary. Year after year, over and over again, I was wasting money and setting the tone for my future.

CHAPTER 4: FIRED

At nineteen years old, reality hit me like a ton of bricks. I was fired from Fisher-Price and I was pregnant; my life was turning upside-down. Goodbye thirty thousand dollars a year plus overtime. Now I was almost in double the debt I'd started with. I was confused and I didn't know what I was going to do. Being fired took a toll on me mentally, physically, and emotionally. I never wanted to feel that way again. It wasn't fair... how could someone give me something and then take it away in the blink of an eye? Where was the remorse? That feeling from being fired wasn't going away and, at an early age, I'd lost all trust in corporations. As the day manager escorted me out of the building, my flesh wanted to fight but my spirit told me to thank him with a smile, so I listened to my spirit. I had a feeling that this had happened for a reason and I was destined for greater things. Those things had not yet manifested, so until then, I had to accept government assistance. Though I did have a little money in my 401k, I cashed out early and ended up paying a fifteen percent interest rate. I couldn't help but ask myself, *"Is this really the American Dream?"* I was living off of credit cards and odd jobs, but I knew that I didn't want to live like that forever. I began musing over the idea of becoming my own boss. It had dawned on me that at every job I'd ever worked, I was unhappy. I always knew that it wasn't enough. I opened my eyes and started noticing the things around me, the buildings we lived in, the cars we drove, the food we ate, and the entertainment we partook in; my future success was staring me right in my face. These businesses were started by someone, someone who was fed up with the norm and decided to seek out ways to improve their lifestyle. If they could do it, then so could I. I knew I needed to find my niche and whatever business I was going to create, it would be a part of my dynasty.

CHAPTER 5: SINGLE MOTHERHOOD

I was now twenty years old, a single mother without a job, and drowning in debt - now what? I remember taking a trip to Hawaii with my mother and my grandmother. While on Fanning Island, we witnessed a man having a heart attack. When he collapsed on the beach and became unconscious, we saw the doctors and nurses working vigorously, trying to save his life, but he ended up dying. That is when my interest in the medical field began. I started researching anything and everything I could find on nursing degrees. I knew how much they made, how long it took to graduate, and which nursing school had the best program. I was twenty two when I decided to attend nursing school, and that is when I really started to plan for my future. I paid my way through nursing school with student loans, but honestly, I could've paid for my education without the loans. The odd jobs that I was working would have been enough money to pay for my classes, but I saw everyone else taking out student loans, so I'd decided to follow suit. I began working as a Certified Nursing Assistant (CNA) at night, but I was only able to work a few nights a week because nursing school was very demanding. Going to school and raising my son (now a toddler) was very exhausting, but nevertheless, I was determined to see it through. My school was about an hour away from where I lived, but I refused to make excuses. I drove back and forth to school every day, leaving early in the morning and coming home late at night. I learned time management; if we were one minute late to class, the doors were locked and we would miss the entire lecture. Although the instructors were very strict, they made sure to instill values into their students. They pushed me to stay focused on my goals. I knew exactly what I wanted for our lives. I was determined to pave the way for my son and leave an inheritance to secure his future. I remembered praying to God for a secure and independent financial future by the time my son reached ten years old, because I knew that it would be the beginning of the most critical times of his life. That is when my hustle became even stronger.

Proverbs 13:22 (NIV) "A good person leaves an inheritance for their children's children, but a sinner's wealth is stored up for the righteous."

There was this thirty five year old woman in my class, with four little children, making straight A's. She was always tired and would constantly express how hard things were at home. I knew that if she could make it, then I could too (even though I've watched some of my friends drop like flies because of the intensity of it all). I made sure to meditate and pray often and I didn't let anything negative get to me. Though I did cry at times, I knew there was a light at the end of the tunnel. I was able to challenge the Licensed Practical Nursing (LPN) boards at the third level of my nursing degree program and I began working as an LPN. The following year, I graduated with my Associates degree in Nursing from Niagara Community College. A year later, at the age of twenty five, I graduated on the Dean's list and with honors (Magna Cum Laude) when I received my Bachelors of Science degree in Nursing.

Chapter 6: Nursing Career Begins

I began working as an extern at Buffalo General Hospital in Buffalo, New York. I was with the Cardiovascular Intensive Care Unit, making fifty thousand dollars a year, plus overtime. That was double my salary at Fisher-Price. I got another car (and car note) while trying to keep up with the same Joneses.... the ones who didn't exist. I traded in my Pontiac Vibe and purchased an Acura TL. In the same exact pattern as before, I was working hard and failed to see any of my money. To make matters worse, I was on the brink of leaving an abusive relationship. My partner, the man who assisted me with taking care of my son while I attended nursing school, began living his life through my dreams. He didn't have any goals of his own. This caused him to have low self-esteem and become very jealous and abusive. I couldn't continue to expose my son to that kind of environment. Even though I loved my partner dearly, his actions failed to prove the same.

CHAPTER 7: THE START OF GAMBLING

At the time of my emotional distress, I was also introduced to the casino. I learned how to play blackjack. I had a beginners winning streak for a while. I would win thousands of dollars at a time and then one day, I started to lose. I felt like I had to play catch up from all that I was losing and I thought I would eventually get back on a winning streak, so I just kept on playing. Here's the problem…I didn't know how to stop. I was high off of the feeling of winning. As if I was a drug addict or an alcoholic, the devil was taking over my life. The casino was my sanctuary; it was where I ran to get away from reality. Nothing else mattered; all I thought about was the casino. I developed friendships with people I didn't know, people who thought that this lifestyle was normal. I even saw famous people and professionals, who our children look up to, consistently gambling. Seeing them is what made me believe my addiction to gambling wasn't that big of a problem. The casino was its own little world, filled with prostitution and drugs; it was a living hell. But they accepted me exactly the way I was and treated me like royalty…or so I'd thought. I received free rooms, shows, rides, food, spas, and drinks. All of these perks were tactics to make me comfortable and keep me gambling. Everything they feel you need is in those walls. They wined and dined me to distract me from the obvious, which is that I was losing. The addiction had gotten so bad that I started maxing out my credit cards, borrowing twenty five hundred dollars here and twenty five hundred dollars there. I was over thirty thousand dollars in credit card debt and about twenty thousand dollars in personal loan debt. On top of that, when you add in my student loans and my car note, I was so far into debt that I thought I would never get out. It had gotten to the point where I almost couldn't pay my rent. I had to ask family and friends for help. I felt like my addiction would never go away, but that was the enemy, manipulating my mind into believing those lies.

Habakkuk 2:7 (AMP) "Will not your creditors suddenly arise? Will they not wake up and make you tremble? Then you will become their prey."

I was the devil's prey and I felt like the Lord had given up on me. I was embarrassed, ashamed, lost, afraid, emotionally and mentally distraught, and neglectful to my child. I was completely out of character, and this new person I had become was sickening to my stomach. I'd stopped looking in the mirror because I knew that I wouldn't recognize the person staring back at me. I needed someone to talk to and tell me what was going on in my life, so I began calling psychics…I was definitely out of control. Over and over again, I was in tears, praying to God and saying, "Please get me out of this mess. I promise that if you do, I will never do anything like this again." My child was losing his mother and I was losing myself. I was living an American nightmare because I wanted to have a glamorous lifestyle, but I was seeking it in the wrong manner. My credit score dropped from seven hundred fifty to five hundred fifteen. I was buried in debt. The same creditors who gave me the credit cards were the same ones harassing me about paying. They didn't have any remorse. My life was a complete mess.

Chapter 8: Revelation

Finally, while I was at the casino, the Lord spoke to me. It was Monday morning, around four o'clock, and I'd prayed all night long before I got there. As I was walking in, I'd noticed that the casino seemed so empty. I felt like I was alone. That is when I realized that I didn't belong there anymore. My body was tired and my spirit was weak. I'd fallen into temptation and enough was enough.

Matthew 26:41 (NLT) "Watch and pray so that you will not fall into temptation. The spirit is willing, but the flesh is weak." (Every weakness you have is an opportunity for God to show His strength in your life.)

2 Corinthians 12:9 (NIV) "My grace is sufficient for you, for my power is made perfect in weakness."

The Lord spoke to me, saying, "Get up and go home now," and I immediately left. I shook the dust off of my feet, ran to my car, and I didn't look back as I drove away. It was like a weight being lifted from my shoulders; my spirit was free from the enemy's stronghold. All I could do was cry. Almost three months after my release, I decided to test my strength. I went back to the casino one last time and played a hand of blackjack. I lost twenty five dollars and instantly felt sick to my stomach. I knew I was finally set free, it was over. I was curious to see what I looked like while in my madness, so before I left, I walked around a bit. I watched a guy lose seventy six thousand dollars in one hour and then call his wife to wire more money. Another guy received a call from his wife saying that they had just lost their house and she was leaving him. I saw the work that the devil created to destroy us, I watched as people won and lost. Not too long ago, I was in this same predicament, and it was destroying me. I refused to judge them for what they were doing, but I felt compelled to pray. Though I was still riddled with debt, I knew that it was over and that the Lord had greater plans for my life. He hadn't failed me; he just stepped back and allowed me to go through it all to rebuild my faith.

Matthew 17:20 (NIV) "He replied, because you have so little faith. Truly I tell you, if you have faith as small as a mustard seed, you can say to this mountain, 'Move from here to there,' and it will move. Nothing will be impossible for you."

I knew He would make a way for me because His love never fails. As of now, I don't look back at this and feel ashamed because I know that I am a living testimony.

Chapter 9: Cycle of Abuse

Shortly after my revelation, I met someone who I fell madly in love with. He proposed, I said yes, and we got married. We then moved to Pennsylvania, and all I could think of was starting a new life with me, my son, and my new husband. I later found out that my husband was emotionally and physically abused as a child by his foster parents. He didn't know who his biological parents were, and that left him with mental and emotional scars. I quickly realized that the more we showered him with love, the further he pushed us away. He also had plenty of debt from college, traffic violations, unpaid bills, and inherited debt from his foster parents. He was mentally, financially, and emotionally unstable. Our marriage was comprised of mental and physical abuse (on his part) and it ended in divorce two years later. I was devastated, but nonetheless, I continued to pray, fast, and meditate on the word of God.

Joshua 1:8 (NIV) "Keep this Book of the Law always on your lips; meditate on it day and night, so that you may be careful to do everything written in it. Then you will be prosperous and successful."

CHAPTER 10: THE START OF "AT PEACE"

I was ready to find my own niche in the entrepreneurial world, but I knew I couldn't do it alone, so I sought out an investor. He was an individual whose family owned and operated a home health care agency in Maryland. It was fate; I initially approached him about a multi-level marketing business, but he looked at me and said "I have something even better." That's when I knew it was time for me to step into my purpose. We had a few meetings, went over the blueprint of our plans, and then our vision for "At Peace Health Care Agency" was created in March of 2009. My partner and I hustled, day in and day out, to get things started from the ground up. In March of 2010, exactly one year later, "At Peace Heath Care Agency" came into existence and it was everything I'd hoped for. I came up with the name "At Peace Health Care Agency" because I was seeking peace for so long, and it had finally come. I put my all into this business; I sacrificed time, invested money, and contributed energy because I was determined to be successful. At the time, I was working at Thomas Jefferson and Genesis Health Care Agency like a slave. I was twenty six years old. I began looking for advice on how to establish a successful business, and that is when I came across the name Dave Ramsey. Dave Ramsey was a financial guru and because I wanted to better manage my finances, I knew I could learn a lot from him.

I began studying his teachings, attending his seminars, and applying what I'd learned to my daily plans. I also learned some of my financial techniques from Suze Orman, mainly on real estate and college planning. After being financially educated, I declared to be debt free by the time I turned thirty. I was determined to live a predestined life of financial health and wealth. Today, "At Peace Health Care Agency" has over seventy five employees and has provided services to over one hundred and fifty clients. Now I am able to invest in other things that'll assist in the continued growth of my empire. I was able to plant a seed and watch it grow and flourish into what I've always envisioned. Through prayer, fasting, and faith, my (amazing) God was able to turn my life around. In November, before my thirtieth birthday, I awakened and had a thought to pull up my credit score. When I did, I discovered I had no more debt. I immediately arose to my feet and began praising Him over and over again. He allowed me to accomplish my dreams. I declared my plans and placed them in the atmosphere, and then God heard them and delivered on His promise.

Jeremiah 32:17 (NLT) "Ah, Sovereign Lord, you have made the heavens and the earth by your great power and outstretched arm. Nothing is too hard for you."

I started asking myself how I could expand on His plan for my life. I knew the seed that was growing would flourish and provide enough harvest to yield and plant more seeds. This was how I saw a way to add wealth to His kingdom, for I know that once you take care of His kingdom, He will take care of yours for generations to come.

Matthew 6:33 (NIV) "But seek first his kingdom and his righteousness, and all these things will be given to you as well."

That's when I learned about the power of tithing. I wanted to control my money the right way because I'd made a promise to the Lord that I would never put myself in the predicament I was in once before. Because of His grace and mercy, I knew that He had control and He would guide me every step of the way.

Chapter 11: The "American Dream"

In this present day, I belong to a few investment groups, own some stocks, and am able to invest in my son's future without hesitation. I'm on a straight and narrow path when it comes to living financially free, and I'm loving it in every way. While going through my trials and tribulations, I started to question the so called "American Dream." According to Google, it is the traditional social ideals of the US, such as equality, democracy, and material prosperity, so then I asked "What is material prosperity?" According to www.englishbaby.com, material prosperity is having plenty of material possessions or things, such as cars, homes, boats, etc. Then I started to think of a way that most people who can't afford to get these material possessions get them. The answer is credit. They are constantly borrowing other people's money and owing them interest, which creates debt. This is the sad thing about it: according to the *Steve Harvey Morning Show*, consumers spend over one trillion dollars on material things. That spending trend is mostly done by African Americans. Why? I believe that African Americans can't get over the roots of slavery. In general, we act as if there's something to prove to all Americans, and to ourselves. We spend our vigor on owning the finer things in life instead of really focusing on priorities (home owning, investing, retirement, and our children's education). Now don't get me wrong, there isn't anything incorrect about wanting the finer things in life, but there is a time and place for everything. I believe it's better earned through hard work, sacrifice, patience, and a plan coupled with a budget. If priorities are placed properly in life, then having the finer things wouldn't be accompanied by a great financial burden. For example: saving to buy a house or working on your credit score should be a priority over buying a new outfit every time you receive a paycheck. Paying attention to African Americans spending trends, the bulk of their finances are spent on material possessions that quickly deteriorate. There are many excuses surrounding why things are the way they are, a primary one being because of the belief that we can't afford them. The problem with this theory is that individuals continue to believe this lie. If you believe you can't afford the finer things in life, then you won't. That is the slave-like mentality working through the African American community. Check cashing companies are solely found in impoverished areas of the city. Why? Because non-white Americans will pay the higher interest rates to cash checks and receive payday loans. I recently heard a story about a man who lost his job at an electric company. He had recently sold his home and received a check for a quarter of a million dollars. A friend of his tried to encourage him to invest in real estate or start a business and he told them, "No, I'm going to go and find me another job instead." This is a classic example of a person with a slave-like mentality. If priorities are placed properly in life, there isn't anything wrong with having the finer things. I started thinking to myself *this isn't a dream, it's an American Nightmare.* The media brainwashes the human mind into thinking that what we see on television is the "American Dream." If we are dreaming, then why do we wake up to creditors ringing our phones off the hook early in the morning and late at night? Every day, they call like clockwork until we agree to make payment arrangements. I consider the media sharks, looking for ways to lure you in. Like bait, they play with you a bit (get you to let your guard down) and then go in for the kill. Media sharks are everywhere, and they constantly devise ways to peak your interest. From the foods we eat to the cars we drive, the clothes we wear, and the phones we buy, they are out to attack us. Look at the Apple hype, which has individuals addicted to buying their products. I believe that they will get up to the iPhone 20 and people will still wait in long lines when they first come out, even if a new phone isn't needed. Open your eyes people and don't believe the hype! The media sharks are biting, and if you allow your sight to be tainted, you will get bitten. I stopped getting caught up in buying the latest fad. I buy what I need; I don't buy what needs me. I need food, but I don't need McDonalds. They need me to keep up their sales. I need shoes, but I don't need Jordan's. They need me to keep up their sales. I need a phone, but I don't need an iPhone. They need me to keep up their sales. You get my drift? Stop buying senseless things that need you more than you need them. Spend less on unnecessary items and start believing in yourself and investing and saving for the future.

Chapter 12: Financial Slavery

Many people are living in an American nightmare called "Financial Slavery." Slavery is a system under which people are treated as property to be bought and sold and are forced to work. In my opinion, Financial Slavery includes the average working American. They wake up to an alarm clock, are told what time to start and stop work, how much money they will receive, when to pick up checks or when they will be deposited into accounts, when and if a raise will be given, what time and how long to take a lunch break, and when to take a vacation. This happens over and over for many years, until the employer says that it's time to retire. When we get into debt, we find ourselves chasing after money just to catch up. Some people surrender and allow the debt to continue to pile up. Many people are spending more time on the job then with their own families. There are only twenty four hours in a day. If you work twelve hours and then sleep eight hours, how many hours do you really get to spend with your family? If you do this four out of seven days a week, then you have three days left to rest and possibly go to church. Where does your family come in on the list? This is one of the major causes of depression, anger, stress, alcohol addiction, gambling, and drug abuse. Many people have mental breakdowns because of it all. I told myself a long time ago that I would not continue to be included in this rat race of chasing after the "American Dream" and becoming a victim to Financial Slavery. I will create my own definition of the "American Dream," celebrating the fruits of my labor instead of someone else's. I will enjoy my life by being my own boss and taking ownership of my destiny. I will break our family's generational curse of Financial Slavery by investing in my (and my son's) future.

Chapter 13: Words of Wisdom

Words of wisdom from senior citizens inspired me to write this book. Sitting and speaking with senior citizens is a pleasure of mine. They have been around for a while and have been tackling life situations longer than I have. I believe that age is a crown of wisdom, and we were all meant to stand-in as living testimonies. One seventy seven year old woman shared her story of accumulating debt. It began with her leasing new cars every two years and having mortgages on properties she couldn't sell because of the value decrease in the housing market. She also acquired debt from credit cards, mortgage refinancing loans, and personal loans. She said she'd thought she was living the "American Dream" until those bills began overflowing. She confided in me her fear of dying while in debt. This wasn't fair and it didn't make any sense. How is it that this woman had given society seventy seven years of her life and she couldn't even enjoy her last years due to the fear of living in debt? She is retired but still works part-time, and all of her money goes towards expenses. She doesn't travel because she can't afford to without using credit cards or getting a personal loan. If retirement is the action or fact of leaving one's job and ceasing work, then why does her story reflect something totally different? There was another woman, a nurse practitioner, who was sixty years old. She was working two full time jobs and still paying off student loans, mortgages, and other debts. I asked her, "When do you have time to enjoy the income you are producing?" She said, "I am immune to working like this; I have done it for over twenty years and I will enjoy it once I retire." Then I met a doctor with his own primary practice, yet (even with his business) he is drowning in debt due to student loans, a beach house, boats, cars, and his children's student loans. He said "I know where I messed up; as soon as I graduated and became a doctor, my wife wanted a house and a few cars. Because I was a doctor, I got approved and put it all on credit. I should've stayed focused on paying off my existing debt and then started working on the home and vehicles. I'm already over two hundred thousand dollars in debt, and now I have two sons in college." Then I met an anesthesiology resident, in his third year, who had a whopping four hundred thousand dollar debt. I also remember the story of another nurse who was in debt because she wanted to impress her in-laws. She, her husband, and their three children were living comfortably in a three bedroom home. However, in being competitive with her in-laws, they decided to buy a bigger home and acquire a larger mortgage. All of her children went to private schools, but her husband worked a low-paying job. She was subjected to working overtime and always complained about living from paycheck to paycheck. Some debt is caused unexpectedly, like hospital bills or a sudden death, but other debts are acquired to gain social status. Be mindful of your spending, stop living in the here and now, and start preparing for the future.

Chapter 14: What is Debt?

Debt is something, typically money, owed or due. It is an amount of money borrowed by one party from another (Google). Many corporations/ individuals use debt as a method of making large purchases that they could not afford under normal circumstances. A debt arrangement gives the borrowing party permission to borrow money under the condition that it will be paid back at a later date, usually with interest (Investopedia).

Romans 13:8 (AMP) "Let no debt remain outstanding, except the continuing debt to love one another, for whoever loves others has fulfilled the law. So Christ has truly set us free. Now make sure that you stay free, and don't get tied up again in slavery to the law."

What this means to me is that when you borrow or use money, you are forced to follow what the lender (slave owner/master) says in regards to paying it back. If he says you owe him one hundred percent interest, then that is what you must pay. For example, say (in 2014) you owed one hundred thousand dollars in student loan debt and you pay one thousand dollars every month. With an interest rate of 6.8 percent, you will be paying the lender, until 2027, the total of the loan and $47,991.00 in interest (http://money.cnn.com/calculator/pf/debt-free/). Why do we allow these lenders to control us and steal our money with our eyes and ears wide open? We are all unconsciously aware of the media sharks every time we turn on the radio and television. There are constantly advertisements persuading us to, mostly, buy and spend. While we are driving in our cars, listening to the radio, and passing by billboards, there are advertisements. While we are watching television, there are advertisements. While we are using public transportation, there are advertisements. They are everywhere, and they are pitching to us, whether we know it or not. There are advertisements for food, clothing, shampoo, perfumes, automobiles, vacations, and attorneys. There are advertisements for other people, such as actors/actresses, hip hop artists, singers, and dancers; they are all walking, talking billboards. The media continues to portray the existence of the "American Dream" and everyone is, unconsciously, fighting to get there. The media shows how all the rich and famous live, how they dress, the foods they eat, and the cars they drive. The difference is, they are paid (and have the money) to do this. The typical American does not have the money but wants to get there somehow, and the easiest way is through credit.

Chapter 15: The System

Debt is very easy to get into but extremely hard to get out of. Why? Because that's what the system is designed to do. Think about it - the minimum age to get a credit card is eighteen. As soon as we're either eighteen, or about to turn eighteen, the creditors are already on us like vultures. This act could be considered a form of mental and emotional abuse. Why? Because the creditors make you feel special when they're offering you a credit card for the first time. When I got my first credit card, I felt like I'd won the lottery. But as soon as you're late on a payment (or two), they bombard you with calls; this causes stress. Most of the time, we receive a credit card and buy expensive things we normally couldn't afford because we think we have time to pay the debt back. There is usually a thirty day window to pay back the amount, without interest. Most people pay just the minimum amount due or pay it back when they are able to, instead of within the thirty days, so then the interest and the monthly payments continue to increase and sometimes, the debt piles up to three times as much as the original purchase.

Chapter 16: Money Lenders

Notice the first thing they say is "Bad credit is okay." Correction - bad credit is not okay. If they are willing to accept your application with bad credit, then you should know that you will be charged the highest possible interest rate. You are, what the lenders consider, a high risk. Money lenders and payday loans are the worst kind of debts, because they have the highest interest rates. They accept anyone, eighteen years of age or older, as long as they have a checking account and a job. This means that if you don't have the money to pay them back, then they have the right to try and garnish your wages. This is a way they can control your checking account, which can cause major problems in the future. Their biggest sell tactics are, "We pay money fast, up to one thousand dollars, and it takes two easy steps to apply." Here is an example of a loan from a company's site (https://www.cashadvance.com/fees).

Loan Amount: $1,000

Loan Length: 30 Days

Amount Borrowed: $1,000

Amount Paid (on your next pay day): $1,150 – $1,300

APR (Annual Percentage Rate): 782% – 1564%

CHAPTER 17: STUDENT LOANS

Financial counseling sessions should be mandatory for anyone applying for student loans. The counseling would evaluate the need for the student loan. A financial advisor would be able to look at the individual's personal finances and determine if student loans are necessary. There should also be high school counselors who assist more with college planning and applying for financial aid. Why? Because there are times where high school students graduate and are unsure of their future plans. The first few years of college are very critical because they set your academic foundation. Unfortunately, first time students fail because they are unaware of the circumstances. Therefore, for some, freshman and sophomore year could be a big waste of time and money. That's why I don't agree with the way the government has built the student loan system. Plenty of people have been brainwashed into believing that money has to be borrowed to attend college and receive a valuable education. I'm here to tell you that this is falsified information. My two year nursing degree cost me twenty five thousand dollars at a community college. I continued on with my Bachelor's degree, which cost eighteen thousand dollars. I was completely finished in three years. When I finished nursing school, my salary was fifty thousand a year, not including over time. My second year, I was making close to six figures with the overtime. If

I would've stayed focused, then I could have paid the student loans off completely, but I was too focused on trying to make more money instead of removing my debt. I was reading an article in *Philadelphia Magazine* recently about a guy who was paying one hundred and ten thousand dollars a year in college tuition for three children (http://www.phillymag.com/articles/my-annual-110000-college-tuition-bill/). Here's the depressing part - a few years ago, there were cases of suicide from college students because of their debt. When I started my business and began to turn a profit, I immediately started to pay back my student loan debt. Some people believe that if you just pay the monthly fees, you're okay. Yes, you are okay as far as making payments on time and being in good standing with the creditors, but you are not okay financially. The interest is still piling up, and that's why so many people feel like they will be paying student loans forever. Hypothetically speaking, they will, unless a plan is in place to get rid of them once and for all. Then there are options of postponing your payments for some time because of financial hardships or if you go back to school. The thing is, you still have to pay the interest, even though the payments are on hold. This means that you are still digging yourself deeper into debt. Then you have student loan consolidation, and to be honest with you, I don't trust anything that says consolidation. Consolidation is the process of uniting (www.merriam-webster.com). Simply put, you are not paying anything off more quickly, you are just uniting all of the loans together into one payment and then spreading them out over a longer period of time, meaning you will be paying that debt longer and paying more interest. I know plenty of people who equate being accomplished and successful with having a bunch of letters after their name. You do not need a plethora of degrees to prove your status in life. It does not define who you are. God does not require you to learn your gifts and talents, they come naturally. As you use them purposefully in the building of his kingdom, he will provide increases. If you feel that the education behind the degree is your lifelong passion or will eventually lead you to your lifelong passion, then by all means, continue to pursue it. If you're currently in a bad position at your job and your degree isn't affording you a higher salary, or assisting you in following your dreams or passion, then don't do it. If you're straight out of high school, you may not know what you want out of life until a year or two afterwards. I strongly suggest community colleges or trade schools because they're much cheaper and you can learn a trade. These are skills you can use as a vehicle to drive you towards your passion. Nursing is a skill I used, and now I am a co-owner of a health care company.

Chapter 18: Home Buying

Don't get caught up in the numbers of pre-approval, those are just guesstimates. They are not the reality of what you would be paying based on your current and future bills. Mortgage lenders have everything look good on paper to make you think that you could afford it, but they neglect to factor in your daily expenses or future plans. Thirty years (even fifteen years) is a very long time, and it is difficult to determine your future income and expenses. Once you get out of debt and decide to buy a home, keep it as an asset. You should always stay within your financial means (what you can afford). It is best to buy a home you can truly afford and not do what the creditors suggest when you are pre-approved. They may offer you a loan approval of two hundred fifty thousand dollars. They say that you will be able to afford it, but can you really? Will you be able to save for retirement (real retirement), save for your children's college plans, take vacations, travel the world, invest in other business ventures, have an emergency stash, and buy the things you feel are necessary? I believe that everyone should have a financial counseling session before they purchase their first home. Not just a home buyers course, but a full financial analysis to determine what you can and cannot afford. In the long run, this will save you money, reduce stress, and decrease the risk of foreclosure. This would be something to consider before you make that big home purchase. A home is supposed to be an asset, not a liability. Also, make sure you do your due diligence when it comes to the property value and the values in the area. Make sure to move into an area where the property value will increase, and not decrease, in the years to come. I don't believe in the concept of refinancing mortgages. To my understanding, you tell the mortgage company that you want to spread out your current loan for a lower payment each month. To me, it sounds as if the mortgage companies have a stronghold on mortgage payments, like a fish on a hook. It allows for people to choose the option of staying in debt longer instead of biting the bullet and paying things off once and for all. I know it hurts, but in the long run, it'll give you peace of mind. Another issue is that some individuals use their refinance money to buy things or pay off another debt. As my grandmother would say, "You are robbing Peter to pay Paul," and then you end up using credit cards or taking out additional loans because you've failed to spend your money wisely. Therefore, robbing Peter was pointless, and you've just made Paul a wealthier man.

Chapter 19: Car Loans

Car salesmen are another group of people who will put some numbers together and tell you how much you can afford without really knowing what's going on in your household. They haven't a clue of your plans for your future; they only live in the here and now. This society has everyone brainwashed into thinking a car loan is needed to purchase a reliable car. That is incorrect. If you took the time out and researched the price of a new car and its value after it leaves the lot, you might reconsider your plans. The value of vehicles depreciates quickly, and you should always be mindful of the cost associated with repairs. With a car payment, even though the value of the car is decreasing by the mile, you are still responsible for paying the original price, plus interest. For example, if you buy a vehicle for fifteen thousand dollars with an APR (Annual Percentage Rate) of ten percent, that means you'll end up paying an additional seventy five hundred dollars over a span of five years. That's a total of $22,500. If you look at the Kelly Blue Book value, your vehicle is now worth ten thousand dollars. Therefore, in five years, the value of your car depreciated by $12,500. What if you have a hardship, like the loss of a job, and it's the fourth year of the car payment? You have been paying faithfully, but now you're no longer able to make the payment. The company you've received the loan from will repossess the vehicle and treat you like garbage, so all of the money you've invested into the vehicle has now gone to waste, and there isn't anything you can do about it because you signed your name on the dotted line. I remember that when I purchased my first luxury vehicle (Acura TL) in 2006, I paid fifteen thousand dollars for it with a car payment. That was a dumb mistake because, at the end of paying the car payments, I calculated everything and I ended up paying almost twenty five thousand dollars. In 2012, six years later, I had to junk it due to water damage that I wasn't aware of and only received five hundred dollars for it. My current vehicle, a Mercedes-Benz, was purchased from a dealer's auction. I paid cash for it and, if I wanted to, I could sell it and get five thousand dollars more than what I've paid for it. I am driving an asset, not a liability, and cars are usually liabilities. Now I believe in auto auctions, because you can check the auction list, do research, see how much a vehicle is worth, and then make a bid. The good thing about them is that most auto auctions require a cashier's check for a purchase, not credit. There are really good deals at auto auctions, but you have to do your homework and have an automobile mechanic check out the vehicle. There are even opportunities where you're able to buy a brand new vehicle. When you are shopping for a vehicle, make a smart decision based on your finances at the time. Don't buy anything over your means. If you have to, then get a car payment as your ultimate (no other way out) last resort, but never opt to lease. Leasing a car basically means that you are renting a car for a period of time and then giving it back. Leases can run from a few hundred to five or six hundred dollars per month. It is like throwing your money in the trash every month, because that is where it is going. You have no rights to ownership of that leased vehicle. If you have that much money to spend each month, then that is the exact amount you can save to buy a used car within a year.

Chapter 20: Bankruptcy

Bankruptcy is a legal proceeding involving a person or business that is unable to repay outstanding debts. The bankruptcy process begins with a petition filed by the debtor (most common) or on behalf of creditors (less common). All of the debtor's assets are measured and evaluated. Upon successful completion of the bankruptcy proceedings, the debtor is relieved of the debt obligations incurred prior to filing for bankruptcy (Investopedia). Bankruptcy is the easy way out of the mess that people put themselves into. Bankruptcy doesn't take care of the mental issues related to debt. I believe that there should be extensive counseling, credit repair, and debt repayment instead of bankruptcy. If all of the debt is wiped away, the lesson cannot be learned. The other day, a woman at the post office told me that she applied for twelve credit cards before she filed for bankruptcy. She did this because she knew that she wouldn't be able to apply for them after her bankruptcy. This means that in a very short while, she will be putting herself back into debt. This society has screwed up the minds of so many individuals by making them think that they have to live with debt. I do not agree with filing for bankruptcy. I believe the individual should pay up and feel the pain, but society knows exactly what it's doing, and that's why there is such a thing as bankruptcy.

Chapter 21: Slave-Like Mentality

To my fellow African Americans, we have to release ourselves from this slave-like mentality. We think that in order for us to be successful in life, we have to work for someone else's dream. Your assumptions limit your creativity. We all have gifts and talents that the Lord expects for us to use. I love the Biblical story from Matthew 25:14-30. There is talk of a master who gives three servants one talent each to multiply. The first two servants increased their talents and were rewarded and the third servant hide his talent and was damned. It is the same for us; we have to use the talents the Lord has planted in us to continue to grow his kingdom and then we will be rewarded. We can do this by praying, meditating, fasting, and waiting patiently, and then we will see our lives changing for the better. We have to stop continuously wondering and asking God why things happen the way they happen. Stop questioning God; things happen that way because it is His will. We cannot control what and who He wants in our lives, and when we go against His will for our lives, issues begin to arise. That's why the servant who didn't return with his talents multiplied was punished and not rewarded. Now there isn't anything wrong with starting out working for others until you get yourself established to build on your own, but you have to plant the seed in order for it to grow. Many of us are saying, "Master, I need more hours," or "Master, can I go on vacation?" Gone are the days of waiting on a miracle. If you are uncomfortable, you have to make yourself comfortable. Don't waste your time and energy on complaining. It's as if we are conditioned to believe that we can't build on our own and cursed with the fear of failure. The world is changing and all of your hopes and dreams are available to you, but you have to want to change your life and do better. If you don't know how, ask someone who does. I associate myself with people who are where I strive to be. Why? Because they're able to share with me their road to success and their testimonies of trials and tribulations. I believe there should be more successful African Americans sharing their testimonies on how they got to where they are and working more with others to get ahead. I believe the slave-like mentality shows up here as well. It appears as if some people are saying, "I have to keep the secrets all to myself or they will take them from me." Is that the primary reason why there are very few (http://www.businessweek.com/stories/2002-06-18/a-slow-walk-up-wall-street-for-blacks) African American owned companies on the stock exchange? Jesus didn't do it alone; he had twelve disciples and many believers. Our company started out with two believers, my partner and I. Now we have over seventy five employees, but we didn't do it alone. We had to work together, build each other up, learn, and grow. The thought of not being able to do it on your own involves examples of mind control, fear, and self-doubt.

Joshua 1:9 (NLT) "This is my command be strong and courageous! Do not be afraid or discouraged. For the Lord your God is with you wherever you go."

If you believe you can be debt free, then you will be debt free and will begin to invest, make more, earn more, and give more. Everything we do is controlled by our minds. What we think is how we react. If you think like you're broke, then you will act like you're broke. If you think like you can get out of debt and live debt free, then you will. If you think you are a millionaire, then you will become one. Break free from living in poverty, it is a sin. Sin is a low living habit; do you see yourself in it? Change your habits. I know it's hard to break them, but if you are used to hanging around people of great complacency, then you too will become complacent. If you are used to working and dreaming, but not acting on your dreams, you will continue to work and dream. If you are used to working on someone else's empire and never begin to work on your own, you will continue to do so. If you want to see change, you have to break those habits. How could you continue to do the same things and expect to see different results? If people are causing you to become stagnant, then you have to remove them out of your life, especially if they are contributing to your stress. Focus on what makes you happy. Self-happiness and self-fulfillment are the keys to a successful life. Other people and material things are only meant to exemplify your happiness, not create it.

CHAPTER 22: CHANGE YOUR THOUGHT PROCESS

Romans 12:2 (NIV) "Do not conform to the pattern of this world, but be transformed by the renewing of your mind. Then you will be able to test and approve what God's will is- his good, pleasing, and perfect will."

We have to think positively about life in general, no matter what. Negativity causes us to fall behind because of the unforeseen changes in our future.

Deuteronomy 28:13 (NIV) "The LORD will make you the head, not the tail. If you pay attention to the commands of the LORD your God that I give you this day and carefully follow them, you will always be at the top, never at the bottom."

We have to pay attention to the positive aspects in life more than the negative ones; negativity causes us to stay stagnate when we are trying to move in a positive direction. The more we think positively, the more positive things will occur. We have to stop allowing other people's problems and issues to dictate what goes on in our lives. We all have times where we are there for others to lean on and offer a shoulder to cry on, but we cannot allow other people's situations to rub off on us or cause us to concentrate on them. What is for them is for them and what is for you is for you. We have to stop diminishing our dreams because of the negative things that occur in life. For the death of a loved one, we have to heal, accept, and find a place to keep them in our hearts and move on. Our relationships have to be chosen deliberately. We have to associate ourselves with more positive, than negative, people. Positive people help us to grow because positive people are moving in a positive direction. Negative relationships drain our time and energy and negative people have goals and values that are moving in a negative direction. I love the saying "Birds of a feather flock together." When you see the success of positive people, you may begin to see things in life differently. That's why it's best for recovering addicts to hang around recovered addicts, so that they can see the light at the end of the tunnel. Most of the time, we allow our emotions to control everything. Everything happens for a reason…everything.

Ecclesiastes 3:1(NIV) "There is a time for everything, and a season for every activity under the heavens."

We can't allow our emotions to be a gateway to our old habits. The devil is trying to keep us focused on the negative, while God is trying to help us get through the storm, learn, and make us stronger from the situation.

1 Peter 5:8 (ESV) Be sober-minded; be watchful. Your adversary, the devil, prowls around like a roaring lion, seeking someone to devour."

1 Peter 5:10 (ESV) "And after you have suffered a little while , the God of all grace, who has called you to his eternal glory in Christ , will himself restore, confirm, strengthen, and establish you."

If a relationship is not working out, trust and believe that God has a bigger and better plan for your future. You have to focus on your strengths more than your weaknesses, because your strengths will continue to build your character and help you grow. At times it may be difficult to see when God is showing us something better, but that is where our faith (and meditation on the word) is prevalent.

CHAPTER 23: SELF-SATISFACTION

Society has brainwashed individuals with what I call "Real Life Hypnosis." Look at all the singers, rap stars, pop artist, actors, etc. All are portrayed for you to believe that you must live, look, dress, and feel a certain way. This is a form of idolism. Idolism is the act of worshipping an idol. Open your eyes and look around; hair weaves, plastic surgery, body enhancements - these are all ways for you to change your image to look like someone else. The hair weave industry is a billion dollar industry. Why? Because many women (and men) are willing to spend their money on ways to make them more appealing to others. Who are you aiming to satisfy, yourself or the people around you? Stop looking for someone else's approval and start uplifting yourself. When people compliment me on the things I wear, I say thank you, but I wasn't expecting to receive a compliment. I wore what I wore because it made me feel wonderful about myself. I'm happy with what the Lord has blessed me with. I don't get wrapped up in what I don't have. I make do with what I do have and remain frugal. Now don't get me wrong, I love designer bags and shoes, but I didn't begin to buy them until I was in a financially stable environment. I made sure that I had cash to pay for them instead of having a bill and drawing up unnecessary interest. I will never forget this story: One day, my partner in real estate and I were looking at properties to purchase. We came across a property we were interested in, so we went to place our bid. There was already another offer on the table, so we sent an email [as a backup] just in case the other offer fell through. We also made sure we noted a cash deal at a little more than the asking price. Thirty minutes later, the realtor contacted us to tell us to submit our offer as soon as possible. Two days later, our cash offer was accepted, and we were able to purchase the property. Cash is king when it comes to getting good deals.

Chapter 24: Budget, Budget, Budget

Luke 14:28 (NLT) "Suppose one of you wants to build a tower. Won't you first sit down and estimate the cost to see if you have enough money to complete it?"

Many individuals have a problem with the word budget. The word budget really means making wiser choices in the present and preparing for a promising future. When budgeting, think short-term and long-term. Short-term deals with today and tomorrow, long-term deals with next year and the following. Thinking only in the short-term is what I call "Not having a budget." You have to plan your future; no one is going to do it for you. Have faith and trust that the Lord has greater things planned for you. Let go of the fear and stop doubting yourself. Always be optimistic about your future. Have you ever heard of the book "The Secret?" It is a book that talks about our energy and how it impacts our lives. If you think pessimistically, your future will be that way. Stop saying what you're going to do and, like Nike says, just do it! Without risk, there is no reward. It is very important to budget our money, live for now, and plan for a peaceful and debt free future. How can this be done? Start off with small steps and gradually work towards big changes. No matter what goes on, time waits for no one. Learn that every time you get paid, every dollar has to have a home. If it has no place to go, then that means it should be invested to make more money until you have a reason for its use. Even the money you use for movies, shopping, entertainment, trips, and dining out has to be budgeted. Why are so many people afraid of budgeting? I believe that society has people afraid that there will not be a future and many people are living for today. But, as Christians, many of us know that Christ is returning. We are not sure of when, but we still have to be responsible and plan for the future. I remember that when September 11, 2001 occurred, I thought the world was going to end…but it didn't. The problem is, tomorrow does come, and many of us aren't prepared for it. I began to realize that concept when I was twenty years old. Now I am thirty one and no matter what goes on in this world, I am getting older and if something happens to me, I have a son to carry on my legacy. I budget because I want to make sure that I can do all the things I'm destined to do for myself and my son.

Chapter 25: Steps to a Healthy Budget

Remember, every dollar you earn has to have a home before you get your paycheck. Before you begin any of these steps, calculate your net worth. Net worth is: assets (properties, income, stocks, bonds, money saved, 401 k) minus liabilities (bills, car payments, expenses, rent, mortgages, etc.). Pull up your credit report to see everything that is owed. For some people, the calculation of assets minus liabilities will be positive and for others, it will be negative. This number is what you would need to work on to get more assets then liabilities. Start recording how much you are spending every month, and on what. This way, you will be able to see where your money is going.

Step #1 Pay Uncle Sam (that usually comes out of your paycheck automatically. If it doesn't, set it up so that it does.) How to do that if it doesn't? Take twenty percent of your income (paycheck, inheritance, royalties, etc., and make sure you check with a tax professional on the percentage that should be) out of your paycheck and put it somewhere you can't touch it. At the end of the year, this will be the amount you will have to pay for taxes. That's how a lot of celebrities get caught up in tax evasion; they forget to pay Uncle Sam when they receive their million dollar checks.

Step #2 Tithe ten percent of your increase. Trust me, tithing works. (This will come first if Uncle Sam automatically takes out your taxes.)

Step #3 Make sure all of your expenses (that need to be paid) are paid:

mortgage, electric, gas, rent, water, and anything else that helps you keep a roof over your head and contributes to your well-being.

Step #4 Please put away some money for emergencies. It should add up to at least three to six months worth of your expenses.

Step #5 Pay yourself. Save a good amount, I would say ten to fifteen percent every paycheck. That way, if anything happens while you're working on fixing your debt, you will have a nest egg to protect you. If you start saving up three to six months of your expenses, you can start to invest that money in the stock market.

Step #6 Work on your debt and pay it down as soon as possible, starting on the debts with the highest interest first.

Step #7 Some people would advise you to transfer funds due on a credit card to another credit card with a lower interest rate, but you have to be very disciplined and mature enough to do this transaction. Don't make the mistake and think that you have extra money to use on the card you transferred the money from. If you make additional purchases on that card, then that will be more debt you will have to worry about later.

Step #8 While you're working on your debt, don't hang out at the mall or any shopping centers if you can avoid it. Before becoming debt free and financially healthy, I use to crave going to the mall to buy clothes, sneakers, shoes, and other things I didn't need. Now I don't have that craving, even though I have enough money to afford it.

Step#9 Think about how much you'll need for entertainment for each month or every two weeks, and set it aside. Most people buy things on impulse, and this will prevent you from staying within your budget. Budget out enough money to do what I call "Celebrating your hard work." These are incentives that are built into your budget to give you a choice to buy what you want.

Chapter 26: Ways to Save Money

#1) Cook more and eat out less. It's healthier and it saves plenty of money. If you're the type who can't cook, budget your money for eating out. Be very realistic and try to eat at places that are healthy and inexpensive. The best time to eat out is lunch time, as most restaurants have lunch specials. For grocery shopping, I love places like Bottom Dollar, Wal-Mart, and Mom & Pop stores because the prices are lower.

#2) When you do cook, make a meal that will last for a few days versus one day. That will cut down on your electricity costs and save you time.

#3) Try auto auctions, online auctions, thrift shops, closet exchanges, etc. Prices for clothing, furniture, shoes, bags etc. will be much cheaper than purchasing items brand new. There isn't anything wrong with vintage pieces.

#4) Try to use slip covers for couches or sofas instead of buying something new.

#5) Want to have fun? There are tons of fun things to do on a budget. Look in your local newspaper or visit your local libraries for all of the free festivities going on in your city. We do discount movies, five dollar movies at Wal-Mart, or go to the library and rent movies for free. You don't have to see the movie when it first comes out. The movie will still be showing the same exact way if you wait a few weeks and your pockets will remain fuller.

#6) Before you shop for clothes, dig in your closet to see what you already have and color coordinate. If I notice that I don't have any gold or grey shoes for the fall, then that's what I will shop for because I know that those are colors that I will primarily wear. I purchase many mix and match items, like shawls, sweaters, basic skirts, and jeans. I also transform fall items into winter items. For example, if I have something in the fall that may need sleeves, I will cover it up with a sweater. In the summer, I wear skirts with flats and sandals, and in the winter, I may wear them with tall boots. I always try clearance first, especially at the end of a season. For example, at the end of summer, I buy sandals for next summer. While in debt, I didn't go to any stores I couldn't afford; that can be very tempting and cause you to go over your budget. I also did closet exchange. I didn't get much for the items I exchanged, but it sure was better than nothing. You can also donate items to the Goodwill and receive a tax credit towards the end of the year.

#7) Whenever you shop for items, such as over-the-counter medications, make sure you get the store brand. Store brands have the same ingredients but cheaper prices.

#8) If you have to pay cash for any dental work, go to the dental schools. The appointments have to be made well in advance but, once again, it is well worth the wait.

#9) Before you make any major purchases, make sure you go home and sleep on it for at least twenty four hours before you make the final decision.

#10) Traveling in groups is always cheaper. Whenever I'm going away on a trip, I weigh out the options of driving, taking the bus, or flying. I shop as early as possible, and I usually use Expedia. I'm a valuable member and I always ask for a rating of three or better. For flights, check for cheap tickets, but you have to be able to either deal with very early or very late flight times. I try to plan my trip well in advance. Unless I'm going to a very important event last minute, I still try to get cheap tickets. I always try to travel on weekends because it is much cheaper. Also, use membership discounts that you are affiliated with, like AAA.

#11) When I have to take a class or go to a seminar, I never choose hotels connected with the class. I always do a little homework to find a place still near, but cheaper. I try to find a friend or relative who may live in the area as well.

#12) I currently don't own any time shares because the fees can add up quickly and go up every year, so there has to be a cost/benefit analysis to weigh that out. If you travel to a particular destination often, then it may make sense for you to purchase a timeshare. Try buying timeshares on eBay, which may be a better solution, but you have to check the fees.

#13) Purchasing a smaller home is better for cleaning and saving on electricity. Also, you won't feel compelled to fill up the empty space with unnecessary items.

#14) While I was working on my debt, we didn't have cable. We used Netflix and the internet only for about five years. Multiply one hundred twenty dollars per month times twelve months times five years. I saved

$7,200. That's a lot of money when you think about it. Nevertheless, television doesn't entertain us much more than the outdoors. We watch movies more than anything. The only reason why I have the bundle package now (at which I talked the cable company into making my bill lower) is because it's a tax write off at the end of the year.

#15) My child doesn't have a cell phone. We use a landline, which is ten dollars per month.

#16) Start a business, it is a major tax advantage.

#17) Pay close attention to your bills. We trust that the companies don't make mistakes when, in fact, they can and will. More than likely, this will cost extra money if you don't pay attention. Also, bills should be paid online. Better yet, sign up for automatic bill pay and it will save you time and money.

#18) Shop around for insurance and get a higher deductible that will lower your premium. This is why you need to save for emergencies - that emergency stash will be able to pay for the deductible if anything happens.

#19) Try to avoid ATM fees. Go to your bank and withdraw money for free.

#20) Try to save on gas by riding a bike, catching public transportation, and carpooling. Weigh out the cost and benefits of doing this.

#21) Cut out bad habits like smoking. I'm not sure exactly how much a pack of cigarettes costs, but that is unnecessary spending on a habit that is killing your health and your pockets. Do the math - if you smoke three packs every week, and it's seven dollars a pack, that's twenty one dollars per week. Multiply by four weeks, that's eighty four dollars per month. Now multiply by twelve, and that is over one thousand dollars per year. Could anyone use one thousand dollars to pay a bill or even two? Absolutely!

#22) Don't try to keep up with anybody else's lifestyle, stay on top of your own. You won't ever be able to live like them, because living their lifestyle was not meant for you. Celebrate who you are and enjoy your uniqueness.

#23) Try to stay healthy by eating the right foods, exercising, and taking vitamins. Remember, being sick can be very expensive and time consuming.

Chapter 27: Discipline

With the current demands in the world, it isn't easy for us to tackle all of the responsibilities in life. Many people ask, "How are you able to stand strong? This seems like a form of punishment or discipline."

Hebrews 12:11 (NIV) "No discipline seems pleasant at the time, but painful. Later on, however, it produces a harvest of righteousness and peace for those who have been trained by it."

Do not conform to the world and stop listening to the conspiracy spoken by others. Set yourself up for some type of reward after a mini milestone. For example, after you pay off one credit card, treat yourself to something you like. After paying off the debt of the third credit card, take a day off of work and do something you really enjoy doing. Your mind set is the key to doing anything. If you set your mind to it, then you will do it. You have to be patient though and realize that God can make a mess into a miracle. If you do your debt-to-income analysis and you realize that it may take you some years to get through it, don't lose faith, stick to it because it is worth it, trust me. You will have a mind at peace when it comes to money. There is an indescribable feeling that takes place once you reach this level of being financially healthy. I love this feeling; it's like a high that I don't ever want to end. You have to knock and if the door doesn't open at first, keep trying because (eventually) it will open. There may be times where you may feel like giving up, but you have to keep trying in order to make it through. Small steps make a big difference. Be true to yourself; don't worry about what others may say, because those who aren't for you are against you. You have what it takes to get through these obstacles. I believe in you.

Chapter 28: The Power of Tithing

At first, I was really skeptical about tithing when I joined a church in March of 2009. I was listening to unbelievers saying rumors about the preachers and listening to stories about what the church does with the tithes, but then I started hearing and reading about testimonies of people who tithed. Then I started mediating on the word and I learned that tithing does work, so I began tithing, little by little, (but not ten percent) and I saw little changes. Then I prayed and continued to mediate and my faith became stronger. Then one day, I gave the whole ten percent and that is when my character, and my life, began to change automatically. I am a living testimony to the power of tithing, and it does work. While going through trials and tribulations, you have to continue to tithe. Things will began to change in your life when you least expect it. Now I'm aiming for the opportunity to give, abundantly, and continue to be a living testimony. Another obvious reason why we should tithe consistently is simple - it's in the word to do so.

Malachi 3:10-12 (NLT) "Bring all the tithes into the storehouse so there will be enough food in my Temple. If you do, says the Lord of Heaven's Armies, I will open the windows of heaven for you. I will pour out a blessing so great you won't have enough room to take it in! Try it! Put me to the test! Your crops will be abundant, for I will guard them from insects and disease. Your grapes will not fall from the vine before they are ripe, says the Lord of Heaven's Armies. Then all nations will call you blessed, for your land will be such a delight, says the Lord of Heaven's Armies."

Plan to use what you have to be faithful and bless someone else. If we take care of the Lord's kingdom, he will take care of us.

Proverbs 11:28-29(NKJV) "He who trusts in his riches will fall, but the righteous will flourish like foliage. He who troubles his own house will inherit the wind, and the fool will be servant to the wise of heart."

Don't put your trust in humans (because no one is perfect) but trust in the Lord.

2 Corinthians 9:8 (NKJV) "And God is able to bless you abundantly, so that in all things at all times, having all that you need, you will abound in every good work."

This means that he will give us everything we need, if we trust in him.

Chapter 29: The Financial Side of Your Relationship

Always love yourself and strive to make yourself mentally, physically, and financially happy in order to have a strong (successful) relationship. We have to put ourselves first on a financial note. This will cause less problems and stress in our relationships. I believe there will be minimal to no arguments about money and finances in the future if this is accomplished. It can be very difficult to let anyone know when you are successful, because some people become intimidated by another person's success. I chose to wait until the appropriate time to release that kind of information. I wait until I truly get to know that person, because that may be one of the main reasons why they stick around. I believe it is necessary to have a partner who will stick by your side no matter what but, at the same time, they're able to have their own dreams, aspirations, and goals in life. Some people want to have a companion that they are able to build a business with and become successful together. Then there are occasions where people are looking for someone to help them get out of their financial mess that they've created. Is that fair to the other person? Absolutely not! It causes more stress on the relationship and it could possibly make the other person feel used. This is what we call a "one-sided" relationship. You have to be financially strong enough to take care of your own mess that you've created. If you're in a financial mess and your spouse or partner recently climbed out of theirs, don't expect them to help you get out of yours. You have to be responsible for the mess you've created. Why? Because if the other person begins to do this for you, then you won't feel the discomfort of paying it off yourself. This will cause your partner to lose trust in you and the financial decisions you make. Being in debt is unattractive because it can make you feel and act like less than who you are! If it doesn't, then that's a problem, because it will seem as if you are comfortable with being in debt. How can you feel comfortable owing and borrowing money you can't afford to pay back? If you could afford it, then you wouldn't have borrowed it. Being in a relationship is also a business; you have to be careful who you're in a relationship with. Your views have to be compatible on your future in a relationship or marriage. It is very important to talk about all previous and current debts including bankruptcies, IRS issues, credit issues, child support, any outstanding loans, and any issues related to money. In order to see if you are compatible, you have to observe each other's actions, judgments, and reactions when it comes to these things while dating. See if the other person will have your back if some type of financial situation occurs. If you notice your partner is irresponsible while dating, then they'll probably be irresponsible if you were to get married. If you notice they are a shopaholic while dating, then they'll probably be the same when you're married. If you notice that they gamble while you're dating, then they'll probably do the same when you're married. Most people don't comment, or ask questions, about the behaviors presented; that could be a major problem. This can be prevented if these issues are discussed early on, while dating. Issues of debt past, present, and future all should be discussed openly and honestly. This will build a solid foundation for your lives in the future. If you and your partner have completely different financial styles, I believe you can teach each other the strengths of both styles, as long as they are financially healthy. By doing this, financial issues will be minimized. While dating, and married, I think it is very important to have separate and joint accounts. This, too, should be worked out prior to marriage. You wouldn't want the IRS coming after any of your accounts because of your spouse's mistakes. Ladies, I know we should be submissive to our husbands and we need to allow them to lead us and be the head of the family, but when it comes to making appropriate financial decisions, women may be more experienced and knowledgeable in that area. We are designed to multi-task. We have to wear many hats: mother, worker, wife, volunteer, social specialist of other's problems, banker, problem solver, chef, hair dresser, lawyer, and the list is endless. That means we may possess the capability to handle things financially in a more appropriate manner unless you know, for sure, that your man can do the task better. By all means, try to figure out who is a master in that area, because it is very important for your future. A prenuptial agreement is a legal contract entered into before marriage that specifies how a couple's assets and debts are divided in case of a divorce. I definitely believe in prenuptial agreements because even though marriage is meant to be forever, life and love still exist and anything could happen. You've worked hard for everything you have; don't let anyone take that away. Protect your assets and your future with a prenup whether you're rich or poor. I have heard so many stories of people being married and it didn't work out, so now all they've worked hard for is taken away by spiteful ex-spouses. Make sure an attorney reviews the prenup to prevent any discrepancies. A friend of mine came up with an analogy that some people are allergic to paper. Some get money, it gets spent, don't want to fill out applications, don't want to buy stocks and bonds, don't want to buy real estate because of the paperwork, don't want to start our own business because of the paper work, don't want to sign marriage or divorce papers. My suggestion is…take some allergy medicine, get your head out of the clouds, and get business minded.

Chapter 30: Knowing One's Self

I hear so many stories from women who've sacrificed doing things in life, such as pursuing an education, taking advancements at jobs or careers, starting a business, etc. for a relationship or marriage that ended up failing. Why? Because we (as women) are designed to sacrifice and care for our family before ourselves. Once we start to realize how much we sacrifice ourselves in that relationship, we become bitter, angry, and confused.

Proverbs 23:7(NIV) "For he is the kind of person who is always thinking about the cost. Eat and drink, he says to you, but his heart is not with you."

We have a heart to trust the person we are in a relationship with more than we trust ourselves. Why? Because when we fall in love, we think that our partner will make us safe and secure. We have to first feel safe and secure with who we are, what we want to do, and who we want to be in life. Start recognizing what's important to you and how much you love yourself. Now don't get me wrong, I love when a man spoils me, provides the finer things in life, and assists me in growing a prosperous future as a partner and friend, but first, I had to concentrate on me having a healthier future. I learned how to love myself unconditionally and make myself happy first. Then I learned the healthier I was, mentally, the healthier my relationship and a marriage could be. That is why you have to make time for yourself. Stop saying that there isn't enough time in the day to spoil yourself. If you can't find the time, then make the time. This is where sacrifice and time management comes into play. Time management can be difficult and can cause some people to give up on their aspirations. Why? Because they think that they don't have enough time to accomplish them. Trust me; success can be achieved if you want it. You have to learn yourself, and your habits, to be able to pay attention to what you can and cannot handle. If you are a night person, why select a day job? That is considered a big waste of time. When I shop, I shop early in the morning to avoid the after work rush hour between five and six P.M. When I travel for appointments, I make them either early in the morning or later in the evening. Even with expenses, I refuse to procrastinate. I take care of them right away; I even have auto-pay on a few of them. I try not to argue with people because we lose valuable time and energy that we will not be able to get back. Most importantly, I always make sure to not allow anyone else to be a waste of my time.

CHAPTER 31: BREAKING ADDICTIONS

Through my trials and tribulations, I have learned that you have to treat yourself with respect. The more you do, the better you will be. This includes mentally and physically, because our bodies are temples.

1 Corinthians 6:19 "Do you not know that your bodies are temples of the Holy Spirit, who is in you, whom you have received from God? You are not your own."

Sin is very expensive and it could end up costing us something priceless - our lives. The devil is constantly at work, and your weakness is his strength. There are many reasons why people can become addicted; genetics, background history, job losses, bad association of friends or relatives, etc. My addiction to gambling was caused by a failed relationship. It controlled my mind, body, and spirit. I didn't recognize who I was becoming, and I was afraid. The Lord always gives us signs of what we're doing, but sometimes we ignore him. Regardless of the fact, because of his grace and mercy, he'll continue to give us chances. That is why I love the Lord; he continually shows me signs until I finally pay attention and have the strength to rebuke Satan and his schemes. I know that while you're going through an addiction, it's not easy to say stop, but you have to have faith and trust and believe that God will bring you through. I remember praying to the Lord and saying,

"I'm released of the demonic spirit, please keep me and cover me and make me a new person inside and out." Addictions not only affect you, but also the people around you. Another form of addiction is excessive spending and buying unnecessary items. Whenever she would want us to clean, I remember my grandmother would say "A cluttered house leads to a cluttered mind," meaning your house is a reflection of you mind. If your house is cluttered, then so are your thoughts. If you have a consumption of unnecessary things in your home, it will be difficult to clear your mind and focus on becoming debt free. There is a name for this behavior, and it is called hoarding. Hoarding is a psychological problem for people who haven't had many things in life (or did at one point) and then those things were, abruptly, taken away from them. These behaviors can have a negative effect on the person's, mind, body, and spirit. It can also affect the relationships they have with other people. This four letter word called LIFE is very challenging, and we may feel that addictions are ways to escape. The truth of the matter is that the Lord is the only way out. I was in denial at first, telling myself, "I'm not addicted, I just like the games," but when I found myself changing, that's when I knew. It was very difficult to do, and through any situation there may seem like no hope, but there is always God. There is always a problem, and as long as you have that "but God," there will always be a solution. Prayer works, and for any addiction, it could be the answer you were searching for. If you see that it is too difficult to handle on your own, please seek professional help. Another step would be to change your affiliations. If you are around people who are the cause of your addiction, you need to move away and break all communications until you are set free.

1 Corinthians 15:33 (KJV) "Be not deceived: evil communications corrupt good manners."

I didn't know what the end results were going to be but, once again, I knew the Lord had something greater planned for my life and I begin to see the vision. Have faith and trust in Him to see you through. The first step will be to recognize (not deny) your addiction.

CHAPTER 32: OUR CHILDREN, OUR FUTURE

Debt, finances, expenses, stocks, bonds, etc. should be discussed with our children as soon as they are old enough to understand the value of money. It takes repetition for anyone to fully understand. When he turned six years old, my son was exposed to me listening to Dave Ramsey's audio CD's on finances. When he turned eight, I made him read Robert Kiyosaki's book "Rich Dad, Poor Dad." I did this at such an early age because I wanted him to grow up being financially savvy. At the age of eight, I also taught him the save, share, and spend method with his allowance. This was one of Ramsey's techniques. Every week, my son would get ten dollars for his allowance. Out of those ten dollars, one dollar would go towards tithing (10% of his increase), he would save four, and spend the other five. I started an online account so that he could view the money that he was saving. I can honestly say that this method actually works. I've noticed that he doesn't spend his money right away; it takes him one to two weeks to spend. In the winter, he has his own business shoveling snow. Sometimes, he'll come home with fifteen to twenty dollars per house. When he turned nine years old, I made him count out seven thousand dollars in cash until he got it right. I also instilled in him the importance of self-worth. He knows not to worry about how any one views him as a person, because everyone else's opinion doesn't matter. Joy within himself, and what he does, is the only thing that should matter in his life. One day, I remember him saying to me, "Mom, I don't like that dress you are wearing!" I said, "I don't care, I do, and I'm wearing it. I am very confident in who I am and I don't care what you or anyone else thinks about my outward appearance. I'm comfortable in my own skin; I don't try to fit in with any worldly crowds, and you shouldn't either. You are already accepted because you are a child of God. You are worth what the Lord has made and instilled in you and you can do anything in life within his will; the sky's the limit. Don't let anyone tell you that you aren't smart enough, handsome enough, or you aren't intelligent enough; you can do anything you put your mind to." I went a little off topic, but he understood where I was coming from. We have to build our children up to be the best that they can be. Whether we like it or not, our children will be responsible for their own future.

Proverbs 22:6 (NKJV) "Train up a child in the way he should go, and when he is old he will not depart from it."

Spending one hundred fifty to two hundred dollars on Air Jordan's is unacceptable in my household. I told my son, "Michael Jordan is not paying for you to go to college, so right now, they're considered a liability, not an asset, unless we can purchase Nike stock and it sores! Now would you rather mommy pay for college or Jordan's?" He said, "We can wait until they go on sale at the

Nike outlet for fifty to seventy five percent off." That was a very smart answer. You have to teach them early on that a liability costs you money and depreciates, but an asset can bring you more money, and it's worth more. Our children need to learn how to become financially healthy. They are the future; they are the ones who will be taking care of us when we get to that age where we are unable to take care of ourselves. Our children should be taught the proper way of building success, genuine happiness, and how to completely love themselves. We are allowing society to, subconsciously, raise our children the improper way. Think about it: the average time a person watches television is five to eight hours per day. If children sleep eight to nine hours a day, and go to school for seven hours, that leaves a few hours for you to raise them. I don't allow my child to indulge in television or video games for more than thirty minutes to an hour on week days. I also monitor what my child watches and listens to as much as I can. Why? Because our children are also victims to media sharks and "Real Life Hypnosis" as well.

Chapter 33: Life After Debt

At first, when I became debt free, it felt a little odd. I had to pause because I didn't believe it. The struggle and fight was over. Out of all the things I promised I would do once I became debt free, I only did a few of them. I was so excited that I was debt free that I became hungry for a new passion; investing. Now I feel accomplished, successful, and a true role model for my child. When I wake up in the morning (or go to sleep at night), I'm not stressed, depressed, or worried about how things will get paid. I feel like I've won because I'm in control of my life, with God leading my every step. I don't have anyone calling and harassing me about any credit cards, bill payments, student loans, etc. I feel at peace with myself and I'm in love with who I am. I have no doubt or fear of my future or where I will be financially. Now I can concentrate on what matters the most to me in my life, my son's future and passing on my knowledge to others.

CHAPTER 34: YOU CAN BE DEBT FREE

Romans 13:8 (AMP) "Let no debt remain outstanding, except the continuing debt to love one another, for whoever loves others has fulfilled the law."

As Dave Ramsey would say, "You have to be sick and tired of it enough for you to want to become debt free." If you want to live a better lifestyle, you have to believe that you can do it. You have to envision yourself being debt free. I remember when I was twenty six years old and first hearing Dave Ramsey. I was in my car, talking to myself and saying, "This guy sounds crazy." But then I kept listening and I started meditating and seeing myself as being debt free. At first, I can admit, I didn't think I would see the day that it actually would happen, but I did. Why? Because I was sick and tired of being a slave to the creditors, banks, lenders, student loan companies, and the government; enough was enough. You have to bring out the courage and faith. Being debt free can be accomplished.

Deuteronomy 15:6 (AMP) "The Lord your God will bless you as he has promised, and you will lend to many nations, but will borrow from none. You will rule over many nations, but none will rule over you."

Is this something your heart desires? You have to be true to yourself and do some soul searching. Your whole heart, body, and soul have to be ready to win at being debt free. I can hear you saying to yourself, *"How I can become debt free when I'm only living on minimum wage or a fixed income?"* While on minimum wage, apply for any and all assistance if needed; food stamps, cash assistance, day care, health care, housing assistance, etc. If you live a lifestyle below your means, you can become debt free. If need be, live with family for a short period of time or find a roommate. I always say to make yourself uncomfortable to get comfortable. When I first started, I moved from a luxury apartment, paying thirteen hundred and fifty dollars a month, to nine hundred and fifty dollars a month. I was in the same school district for my son and I saved four hundred dollars a month. It wasn't the greatest, but within those two years, I saved $9,600 dollars. You have to evaluate your current situation and, by all means, anything to save money to set yourself up for your future. Make sure the place you live, and all your bills, are within your means. For example, if you are making minimum wage, why do you have an iPhone? Once you get all your bills covered under your minimum wage job…get a second job. But once you get the second job, don't get a better place to live or buy nicer things, not yet. First, follow your budget and start to pay all of your outstanding bills, including student loans, car loans, credit cards, everything. Get a copy of your credit report from all three bureaus: Experian, Equifax, and Transunion. List everything: medical bills, outstanding loans, etc. I know this may hurt, but you've caused this, so you have to feel the pain. If there is something on your credit report that doesn't belong, call the credit bureaus to find out what is going on immediately and find out how to dispute it. I have experienced credit fraud first hand, and you shouldn't be paying for someone else's debts. Now, start paying off the bills with the highest interest. Why? Because you will want to get that down to owing only half, and then start paying the next one. The same cycle should be repeated until your debt is paid off. When paying off debt, always look for better deals. While I was paying off my student loans, I was offered a 1.99 percent APR with no transfer fee. At the time, I was paying a 6.8 percent APR. This transfer saved me a difference of fifty cents per day (fifteen dollars per month). Once I paid off more debt, and my credit got better, I was offered a zero percent interest rate with a four percent transfer fee. Call the student loan companies, credit card companies, personal loan companies, etc., and ask them how to reduce your interest without consolidation. Have faith, trust in God's plan, believe in yourself, and stay focused on your own business and not anyone else's. If you're older than thirty, I believe you can still become debt free. You may have to make more sacrifices in order to obtain that goal, but you can still do it. You have to begin with seeing your habits and having the will to change them. People say that, as we grow older, we become set in our ways. Well, you have to seek out the habits in your life that caused you problems and make up the decision in your mind to change and find a solution. Let's say that you are used to playing the lottery every day. That's ten dollars a day for the last thirty years.

It may be very difficult for you to stop that habit. You will have to change your mindset and decide not to continue investing in that system. Those ten dollars a day, for thirty years, equals seventy two thousand dollars. Congratulations, you have just paid someone's annual salary for a few years. You have to set yourself up for debt relief and get to where you feel comfortable, confident, and at peace.

Summary

The main focus point of this book was to tell you that being debt free is possible. Through my trials and tribulations, I was able to overcome. I wasn't born with a golden spoon in my mouth. Everything I have was the result of me working hard. I paid for everything myself: school, cars, housing, clothes... no one in my family had the means to support me financially, but they were able to offer love and support with caring for my son. The Lord blessed me with the ability to, now, have a strong personal and spiritual foundation. Through my challenges, I've learned that I had to take some steps back in order to get ahead. Through the process of becoming debt free, I have learned: don't make any financial decisions after a failed relationship, death of a loved one, or divorce. Your mind is very powerful and it will wander into things you would have never imagined. Give yourself time to heal. Before making any home purchases (or financial moves) pray, meditate, and ask the Lord for guidance; with patience, he will see you through. I was very blessed to be able to go through my trials and tribulations and share my story with those of you who are in debt. I hope that my testimony will, indeed, help others who are going through the same things that I've gone through. I hope that this book will help you to reach your goals of becoming financially healthy and give you a better outlook on your future. It is very important for us to get this information through to the younger generation. I wish there was someone who would have guided me in the right direction when it came to finances, but there wasn't, and that is why I am here, sharing my struggles and my breakthrough. I beseech you to pass on this book to the next generation as a gift to a family member or friend who would benefit from this greatly. Let's start a movement and show everyone how to live a financially healthy and debt free lifestyle.

ABOUT THE AUTHOR

Growing up in Buffalo, a small city in upstate New York, I didn't live in a single family home surrounded by a white picket fence with my mother and father. I wasn't raised with a golden spoon in my mouth and a nanny to attend to my every beckoning call. But instead, I grew up around individuals with low paying (to no paying) jobs, drug dealers, food stamp users, Women Infant Child (WIC) program participants, and public assistance seeking individuals. It would have been easy for anyone to fall victim to complacency, but following the norm was never one of my strong suits. I've watched my mom work extremely hard as a single woman, and though we were susceptible to the struggle, she was able to take care of my brother and I, pay the rent, bills, and offer a little fun from time to time. As Tye Tribett would say, life was good in the hood. I love and appreciate my mom's hustle and struggle. It's not easy raising a child, let alone two children, but she made it through. Without struggles, there aren't any true rewards. Now I am thirty one years old and I wear many hats throughout the day. I am a child of God, Mother, registered nurse, co-owner of "At Peace Health Care Agency," missionary, a member of the National Association University of Women Philadelphia Suburban Branch, a member of two investment clubs, an up-and-coming fashion designer, and now an author. My brother and I are both successful. Though my dad wasn't around very often, I was able to overcome that obstacle of an absentee father and break away from being a statistic. Despite your past, you have the power

CPSIA information can be obtained at www.ICGtesting.com
Printed in the USA
BVOW05s1730240715

409830BV00002B/3/P